∗ HISTORY STARTING POINTS ∗

JULIUS CAESAR
and the
ROMANS

DAVID GILL

W
FRANKLIN WATTS
LONDON • SYDNEY

Franklin Watts

First published in Great Britain in 2016
by The Watts Publishing Group

Copyright © The Watts Publishing Group 2016

Series editor: Julia Bird
Editor: Sarah Silver
Series designer: Matt Lilly
Picture researcher: Diana Morris

ISBN 978 1 4451 4711 6

FSC
www.fsc.org
MIX
Paper from
responsible sources
FSC® C104740

Printed in China

Franklin Watts
An imprint of
Hachette Children's Group
Part of The Watts Publishing Group
Carmelite House
50 Victoria Embankment
London EC4Y 0DZ

An Hachette UK Company

www.hachette.co.uk
www.franklinwatts.co.uk

CONTENTS

Meet Julius Caesar ⸺⸺⸺ 4

Julius Caesar's life story ⸺⸺ 6

The Roman Republic ⸺⸺⸺ 8

Roman games ⸺⸺⸺⸺ 10

The Roman army ⸺⸺⸺ 12

Caesar: The great general ⸺⸺ 14

Caesar in Britain ⸺⸺⸺ 16

Civil war ⸺⸺⸺⸺⸺ 18

Cleopatra ⸺⸺⸺⸺⸺ 20

Caesar the dictator ⸺⸺⸺ 22

The start of the Roman Empire ⸺ 24

How do we know? ⸺⸺⸺ 26

Caesar's legacy ⸺⸺⸺⸺ 28

Timeline ⸺⸺⸺ 30

Glossary and quiz ⸺ 31

Index and answers ⸺ 32

MEET JULIUS CAESAR

Almost everyone has heard about the ancient Romans, how they lived and how they created a vast **empire**. Julius Caesar was one of the most famous Romans. His name, Caesar, became the title by which all Roman emperors were known.

This bust of Julius Caesar can be seen at a museum in Naples, Italy.

Who was Julius Caesar?

Gaius Julius Caesar was born into a wealthy and important family in Rome. Some of his ancestors had held top jobs in the Roman **Republic**. Caesar's father was the **governor** of a Roman province that is now part of Turkey.

The senate met to make important decisions. Before Caesar became a dictator the senate held the power of government.

When did Julius Caesar live?

Julius Caesar was born in 100 BCE. All through Caesar's life Rome was a republic, which meant it was governed by the **senate** (see page 8). By the time Julius Caesar was 50 years old the Romans had **conquered** much of Europe. Julius Caesar was **assassinated** in 44 BCE when he was 55 years old.

Where did Julius Caesar live?

Julius Caesar was born in Rome, the biggest city in the world at the time. He was educated in Rome and also in Greece, where he went to a school of **philosophy**. Most of Caesar's life was split between Rome, where he worked in politics, and Spain and France, where he led the army to expand and protect the Roman Republic. Caesar also lived in Turkey, Italy and Egypt.

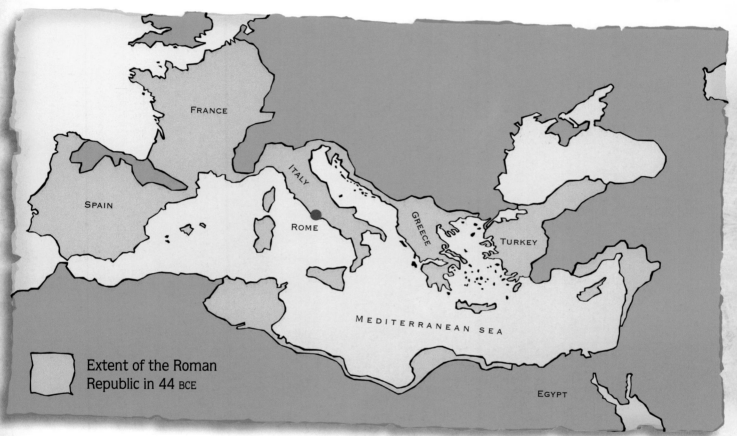

FRANCE

SPAIN

ITALY

ROME

GREECE

TURKEY

MEDITERRANEAN SEA

Extent of the Roman Republic in 44 BCE

EGYPT

Why is Julius Caesar famous?

Julius Caesar was a great **general** who won many battles for Rome. He is famous for conquering Gaul (France) and trying to invade Britain, not just once but twice. When Caesar marched on Rome in 49 BCE, he started a **civil war** that led to the end of the Roman Republic and the beginning of the Roman Empire. In 1599, English playwright William Shakespeare wrote a play about the tragic and violent death of Julius Caesar. This famous play helped to keep the memory of Caesar alive.

JULIUS CAESAR'S LIFE STORY

Although Julius Caesar was born into a rich and noble family, it was not certain that he would become a great leader. It was Caesar's determination to be in charge that helped him get to the top, but it also led to his downfall.

1

WHEN JULIUS IS BORN HIS MOTHER HAS AN OPERATION ON HER STOMACH. THIS METHOD OF CHILDBIRTH IS NOW CALLED A CAESAREAN SECTION.

2

EIGHTEEN YEARS LATER, ROME'S RULER ORDERS CAESAR TO DIVORCE HIS NEW WIFE BUT HE REFUSES AND THEY FLEE ROME.

3

CAESAR IS 19 WHEN HE WINS THE 'CIVIC CROWN' FOR SAVING THE LIFE OF A ROMAN CITIZEN.

THIS IS THE HIGHEST HONOUR.

4

I DRESS TO IMPRESS.

CAESAR LOVES TO BE FASHIONABLE AND MAKES SURE HE GETS NOTICED BY EVERYONE HE MEETS.

5

THIS MAN IS INNOCENT AND I WILL PROVE IT.

AT 23 CAESAR DEFENDS A FAMOUS CRIMINAL IN A BIG TRIAL. HE IS AN IMPRESSIVE SPEAKER.

6

WHEN CAESAR IS CAPTURED BY PIRATES HE TELLS THEM TO DEMAND MORE MONEY FROM HIS FAMILY.

ASK 20 TALENTS FOR THIS ONE.

I AM WORTH MORE THAN THAT.

7 CAESAR, NOW 40 YEARS OLD, IS VOTED 'CONSUL OF ROME'. IT IS A SIMILAR JOB TO BEING PRIME MINISTER.

8

AS GOVERNOR OF GAUL (FRANCE) CAESAR LED HIS ARMY AGAINST DIFFERENT TRIBES TO BRING THEM UNDER HIS CONTROL.

9

AT THE AGE OF 45 CAESAR BECOMES THE FIRST ROMAN LEADER EVER TO LAND IN BRITAIN.

10 AT 50 CAESAR ENTERS ROME WITH AN ARMY BUT HIS ENEMIES HAVE FLED, FEARING WAR.

11

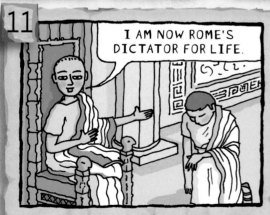

CAESAR PERSUADES SENATORS TO MAKE HIM THE LEADER OF ROME, A BIT LIKE BEING KING.

12 ONLY TWO YEARS LATER, WHEN HE IS 55, FORMER FRIENDS AND ENEMIES OF CAESAR ASSASSINATE HIM ON MARCH 15.

THE ROMAN REPUBLIC

By the time Julius Caesar was born the republic had been going for almost 400 years. The people of Rome were very proud that they were not ruled by one person, but by a council of senators in the senate.

How the republic worked

The Roman Republic was organised in a way that stopped power getting into the hands of a few people. Those with the greatest power were senators. You could only become a senator if you were over 30 years old and owned lots of land. All the other jobs were elected by male Roman citizens.

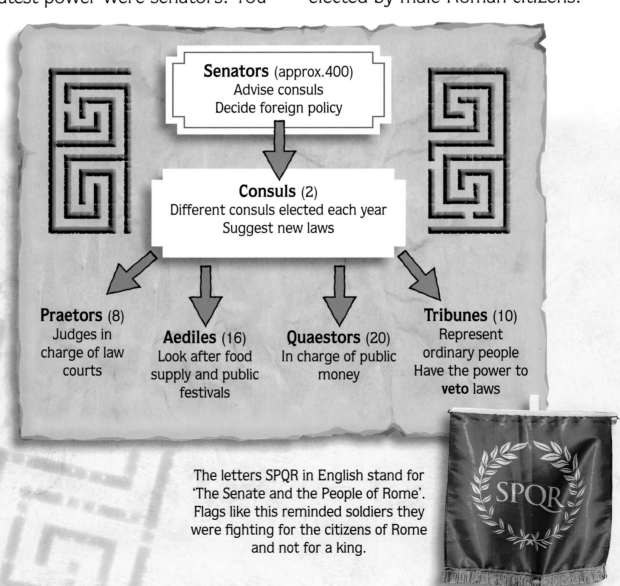

Senators (approx.400)
Advise consuls
Decide foreign policy

Consuls (2)
Different consuls elected each year
Suggest new laws

Praetors (8)
Judges in charge of law courts

Aediles (16)
Look after food supply and public festivals

Quaestors (20)
In charge of public money

Tribunes (10)
Represent ordinary people
Have the power to **veto** laws

The letters SPQR in English stand for 'The Senate and the People of Rome'. Flags like this reminded soldiers they were fighting for the citizens of Rome and not for a king.

HISTORY ⛓ LINKS

THE UNITED STATES OF AMERICA COPIED SOME OF THE WAYS IN WHICH THE ROMAN REPUBLIC WAS GOVERNED. AMERICANS ELECT SENATORS WHO MAKE LAWS IN THEIR SENATE CHAMBER. THE **LATIN** WORD 'SENATUS' MEANS A COUNCIL OF OLDER, WISE MEN.

Getting the top job

Julius Caesar knew that if he was to succeed in life he had to get elected to the post of consul. In this role he would have many powers, including control over the army. But first Caesar had to be elected to the less important jobs (see the diagram on page 8) and that meant being noticed by both rich and poor.

Here are three ways Julius Caesar got himself noticed:

1. Look great
Caesar wore clothes that were just a bit different to everybody else. He made people notice him by setting the fashion. Caesar definitely had the wow factor.

2. Be popular
Caesar became really good at making speeches in public. He could make people laugh and cheer for him and he could persuade them that his ideas were the best ideas.

3. Make friends with important people
Caesar made friends with Pompey, a great hero who had won many battles for Rome, and Crassus, a very rich politician who lent Caesar lots of money.

Crassus is thought to be the wealthiest man in Roman history.

9

ROMAN GAMES

Across ancient Rome, crowds flocked to watch shows held in amphitheatres, theatres, stadiums and circuses.

Who paid?

Roman emperors and other important people paid for public entertainments. Organising free entertainment was a way of celebrating religious festivals and victories in war. It also helped keep the general public happy. Julius Caesar organised games in Rome when he was an aedile (see page 8). He borrowed money to make the games memorable. All 500 gladiators wore silver armour which reflected the sun into the audience, dazzling the spectators.

The Romans built public buildings, including this amphitheatre at Umm Qais in Jordan.

Two gladiators face each other on this Roman pot found at Colchester, Essex.

FASCINATING FACTS

THE BEST GLADIATORS TRAINED AT SPECIAL FIGHTING SCHOOLS AND COULD BE FAMOUS IN THE SAME WAY AS FOOTBALL STARS ARE TODAY. ORIGINALLY GLADIATORS WERE **SLAVES**, CRIMINALS OR PRISONERS OF WAR. LATER, SOME PEOPLE ACTUALLY CHOSE TO BECOME GLADIATORS.

Bloodthirsty shows

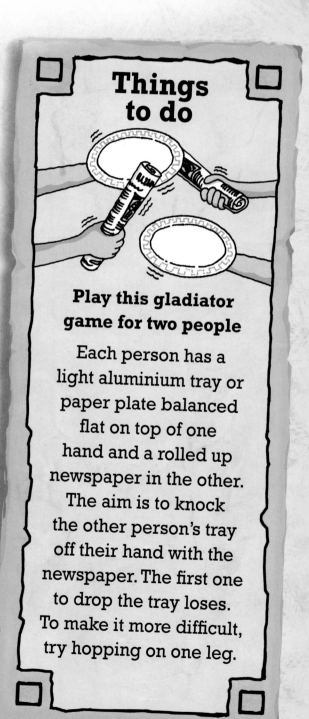

A gladiator's sword

Roman people enjoyed watching people and wild animals fight for their lives. Gladiators fought other gladiators, or used their skills to kill wild animals. Sometimes thousands of animals were killed as entertainment. And the Romans didn't stop at killing animals for sport but also staged shows where criminals were **executed** in front of the crowd.

Chariot racing

Chariot racing was also a very popular sport. The most famous race track was the Circus Maximus in Rome. The stadium could hold 150,000 people. In 46 BCE, Julius Caesar extended the track so that one circuit was about a kilometre in length. Anything from four to ten chariots raced against each other for seven circuits. It was a dangerous but exciting spectacle.

A racing chariot is captured on this 4th century Roman mosaic showing chariot racing at the circus in Barcelona, Spain.

Things to do

Play this gladiator game for two people

Each person has a light aluminium tray or paper plate balanced flat on top of one hand and a rolled up newspaper in the other. The aim is to knock the other person's tray off their hand with the newspaper. The first one to drop the tray loses. To make it more difficult, try hopping on one leg.

When Julius Caesar died in 44 BCE, Rome controlled nearly all the land around the Mediterranean Sea. The Roman Republic had defeated every country it had fought. It was able to do this because it had the most disciplined soldiers, armed with the best war machines in the world.

Legionaries

Legionaries were infantry or foot soldiers and they formed the main part of the army. They were all Roman citizens. A legionary wore armour over his tunic, a helmet and leather sandals, and he carried a rectangular shield made from layers of wood. His weapons were a javelin and a short sword used in close fighting. Caesar's legionaries trusted him because he had won many victories.

Re-enactors dressed as legionaries.

My own research

A centurion in the Roman army was in charge of a century (see page 13). He was roughly equal to the rank of a captain in a modern army. Use library books and the Internet to find out the ranks in a modern army and put them in order.

Auxiliaries

Auxiliaries were made up of men from foreign lands ruled by the Romans. Julius Caesar recruited specialist fighters, such as horsemen from Spain and archers from Persia (modern Iran). An auxiliary was made a citizen of Rome after serving in the army for 25 years.

Organising the Roman army

The Romans were fantastic at organising every part of Roman life and that included the army. Legionaries knew exactly what they had to do when it came to fighting a battle. The number of soldiers shown in these boxes are only approximate, as men regularly died in battle or from disease and were not always replaced. Note that a century was eighty men, not a hundred.

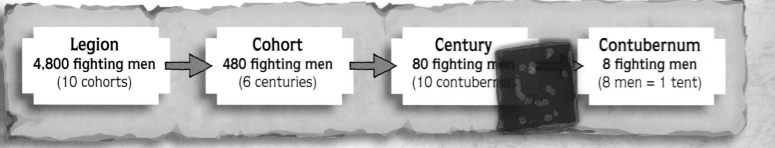

| **Legion** 4,800 fighting men (10 cohorts) | **Cohort** 480 fighting men (6 centuries) | **Century** 80 fighting men (10 contubernia) | **Contubernum** 8 fighting men (8 men = 1 tent) |

War machines

The Roman army had the very best war machines which made use of the latest technology. Many armies did not want to face Roman legions in an open battle, so they stayed inside a fortress, behind walls or a wooden fence. This meant the Roman army needed **siege** weapons to break through.

An artist's impression of the Roman army using siege weapons.

CAESAR: THE GREAT GENERAL

Between the ages of 41 and 55, Julius Caesar was away from home. For all of that time he was in charge of an army, fighting battle after battle. In those years, Caesar made his reputation as one of the greatest generals of all time.

Caesar's war commentaries

In 58 BCE, Caesar was made governor of Gaul. He made sure everyone back home knew about his great victories by writing them down and having his accounts read out in the streets of Rome to crowds of ordinary citizens. Caesar was their hero! In the extract (right) he describes a battle against **tribes** from Germany.

"When the signal was given our men moved forward to attack. But the enemy rushed forward so suddenly that there was no time for throwing the javelins at them. We threw them aside and fought with swords hand-to-hand. Then the Germans moved into a formation with their spears out, protected by a wall of shields. Many of our soldiers leapt on top of the Germans and with their hands tore away the shields, and wounded the enemy from above."

A Roman coin (48-47 BCE) commemorating Caesar's conquest of Gaul.

HISTORY LINKS

JULIUS CAESAR WAS NOT THE ONLY LEADER TO WRITE A HISTORY OF THE WARS HE FOUGHT. WINSTON CHURCHILL, PRIME MINISTER OF GREAT BRITAIN FROM 1940–45, WROTE A HISTORY OF THE SECOND WORLD WAR.

The Battle of Alesia

In 52 BCE, Vercingetorix, a tribal leader, had persuaded the tribes of Gaul to fight Caesar's army. Caesar tracked Vercingetorix all the way to Alesia, a well-defended fort on top of a hill. Once there, Caesar had his soldiers build a huge, 16-km-long wooden fence all the way round Alesia to trap the Gauls and starve them out. Then Caesar built another, even longer fence to protect his troops from attack by Gauls who were coming to rescue Vercingetorix. The fighting was furious, but in the end Caesar won a stunning victory. From then on, Caesar had very few problems with the Gauls.

Reconstruction of Roman fences from the Battle of Alesia, in Burgundy, France

Things to do

Read this extract from Caesar's own account of the Battle of Alesia. What might Caesar have written next? Continue his description of the battle. Make it exciting and heroic for the people back in Rome.

"The Gauls, protecting themselves with shields, built up the earth against the palisade (fence) so they could reach the top and climb over... I put on my red cloak and hurried to the men."

CAESAR IN BRITAIN

Romans believed Britain lay at the edge of the world. They were fascinated by stories they had heard about this curious land inhabited by a strange people with their 'weird ways'.

Caesar invades Britain (twice!)

Julius Caesar invaded Britain in 54 BCE and again the following year. The first attempt was probably just a scouting mission to find out the strength of the British. But in 55 BCE Caesar returned with a large army.

There were 16,000 troops and 2,000 **cavalry**. His second attempt to conquer Britain failed because he met with fierce fighting and was forced to return to Gaul to put down a **rebellion** there.

Why did Julius Caesar invade Britain?

1. He wanted the glory that came with conquering a new land.

2. He believed Britain had lots of gold, silver and tin.

Things to do

Use this map and an atlas to name four countries ruled by the Roman Republic.

See page 32 for answers

ATLANTIC OCEAN

BLACK SEA

MEDITERRANEAN SEA

Extent of the Roman Republic in 44 BCE

Caesar lands on the edge of the world

An artist's impression of Caesar landing in Britain in 55 BCE.

When news of Caesar's invasion reached Rome, senators ordered 20 days of celebration. They were thrilled to think Julius Caesar had tamed such a wild place. They were too far away to know the truth. Caesar wrote all about his invasion of Britain. We can still read his thoughts 2,000 years later!

FASCINATING FACTS

THE ROMANS DID SUCCESSFULLY INVADE BRITAIN IN CE 43. THE EMPEROR CLAUDIUS PARADED THROUGH THE STREETS OF COLCHESTER WITH ELEPHANTS BROUGHT OVER FROM EUROPE.

What Caesar wrote about British warriors

"To start with they drive their chariots all over the field of battle and throw their javelins. Men jump from the chariot and fight on foot. The chariots return to give a way of escape if things do not go well."

What Caesar thought about Britain

"They use brass or iron rings of the same weight as their money. There is timber of every sort and the number of cattle is great. They do not think it lawful to eat the hare or goose. Most of the people live on milk and meat. They do not grow corn. They dress in animal skins. They shave their bodies but wear their hair long and grow hair on their upper lip."

CIVIL WAR

By law generals were not allowed to cross the Rubicon and approach Rome with an army in case it threatened the Roman Republic. But in 49 BCE, Caesar crossed the Rubicon with his entire army. He had passed the point of no return.

The Rubicon river, about 300 km to the north of Italy, marked the border between Rome and its provinces.

Reasons for civil war

Caesar had finally conquered Gaul and wanted to return to Rome, but there was a problem. His enemies wanted to put Caesar on trial for crimes they said he had committed when he was consul. Pompey, a famous general, had joined Caesar's enemies. Caesar believed his life was in danger, so he refused to enter Rome without his army. The two sides were heading for civil war.

CIVIL WAR BROKE OUT IN BRITAIN IN 1642 AND LASTED UNTIL 1649. SUPPORTERS OF THE RIGHTS OF PARLIAMENT, LED BY OLIVER CROMWELL, CLASHED WITH SUPPORTERS OF KING CHARLES I. KING CHARLES I WAS BEHEADED IN JANUARY 1649. HE IS THE ONLY BRITISH MONARCH EVER TO HAVE BEEN EXECUTED.

An artist's impression of King Charles I being led to his execution.

Caesar vs. Pompey

Caesar

Pompey

Caesar and Pompey were two of the greatest Roman generals. They had once shared the same family when Pompey married Caesar's daughter, Julia, but she had died four years before. Now Caesar and Pompey were on opposite sides and neither of them wanted to back down from a fight. But the fight would be between two armies, not just two people.

The battle of Pharsalus

In 48 BCE, the armies of Caesar and Pompey finally came face to face, not in Italy but in Greece. Pompey did not really want to fight. He knew Caesar's men had very little food left and were close to starvation, but senators forced Pompey to stay and fight. Although Caesar had only half the men of Pompey's army but he still won. He was a military genius!

FASCINATING FACTS

POMPEY ESCAPED FROM THE BATTLE OF PHARSALUS AND FLED TO ALEXANDRIA IN EGYPT, WHERE HE WAS ASSASSINATED AS HE CAME ASHORE. WHEN CAESAR WAS SHOWN THE HEAD OF POMPEY, IT WAS SAID THAT HE CRIED. THOUGH ENEMIES, THEY HAD ONCE BEEN FRIENDS.

CLEOPATRA

Caesar pursued his enemy Pompey all the way to Alexandria in Egypt. When he reached Alexandria, Caesar met and fell in love with Cleopatra, the Egyptian queen.

The River Nile

Egypt: the 'bread basket' of Rome

Egypt was very important to Rome because it supplied most of its grain for making bread. If the harvest in Egypt failed, Romans would go hungry. Much of Egypt was desert, but the land alongside the River Nile was very **fertile**.

Cleopatra: a beauty queen?

Cleopatra is famous for her beauty, but perhaps her attraction was not just down to her looks. People who knew her said she was clever and funny. She had charm and could be cunning. She certainly knew how to get Caesar's attention. At their very first meeting she smuggled herself into his room inside a laundry bag.

FASCINATING FACTS

CLEOPATRA WAS NOT EGYPTIAN. HER FAMILY CAME FROM MACEDONIA, NORTH OF GREECE. CLEOPATRA WAS THE LAST EVER PHARAOH OF EGYPT.

Cleopatra on a gold coin

Love and war

After Caesar's death, Cleopatra also had a love affair with Caesar's close friend, Mark Antony. She had children by both men. Mark Antony upset many Romans by living with Cleopatra in Egypt when he was already married to Octavia, sister to Octavian, the man who would become Emperor Augustus (see page 25). Octavian declared war on Cleopatra in the hope of getting rid of both her and her lover, Mark Antony.

Cleopatra and her son Caesarion, named after his father, Caesar.

A tragic end

Octavian's army met Mark Antony at the Battle of Actium in 31 BCE. Mark Antony's fleet of ships was destroyed and so he returned to Egypt, where he killed himself. When Cleopatra heard of his death she committed suicide, either by allowing a poisonous snake to bite her or by swallowing a snake's venom.

The venom of this Egyptian cobra is released through its fangs. It can cause death by preventing people from breathing.

21

CAESAR THE DICTATOR

A dictator is someone who has total power. When Caesar defeated Pompey he was made 'Dictator' by the Senate because the country was in a crisis. He was only supposed to be dictator for a short time, but Caesar had no intention of giving up any of his powers.

Caesar, Dictator of Rome

Senators hated the idea of one man having total control of the country. They believed it was better to have a council of wise men who would make the laws and decide foreign policy. But the Roman people just wanted peace and, if Caesar could give them peace, then who cared if he made himself Dictator of Rome?

My own research

Julius Caesar changed the calendar so it had 365 days plus one extra day every four years. He also introduced twelve months rather than ten. Use library books and the Internet to find out which months are named after Roman gods and which month Julius Caesar gave his name to.

A Julian calendar with months, weeks and days marked by pegs.

What do you think?

Read the sentences below and decide whether Julius Caesar was a good or a bad dictator.

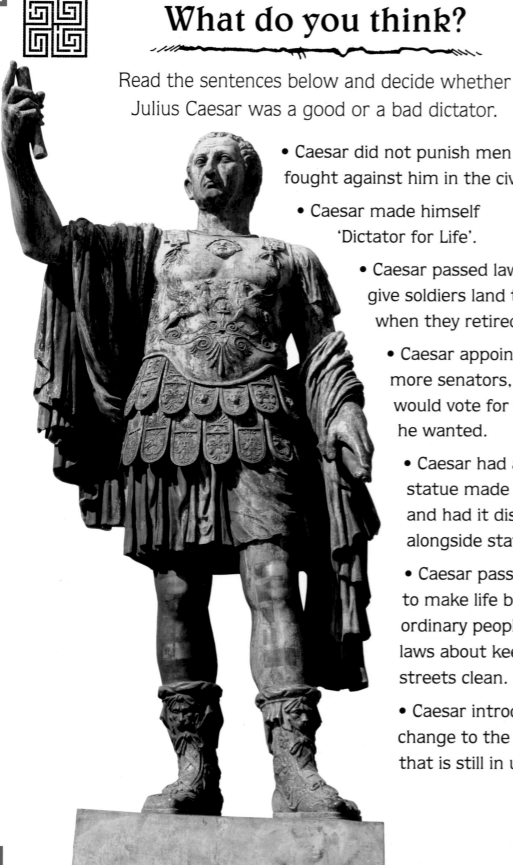

- Caesar did not punish men who had fought against him in the civil war.

- Caesar made himself 'Dictator for Life'.

- Caesar passed laws to give soldiers land to live on when they retired.

- Caesar appointed hundreds more senators, men he knew would vote for what he wanted.

- Caesar had an ivory statue made of himself and had it displayed alongside statues of gods.

- Caesar passed laws to make life better for ordinary people, such as laws about keeping streets clean.

- Caesar introduced a change to the calendar that is still in use today.

THE START OF THE ROMAN EMPIRE

Many senators thought Caesar had too much power as Dictator. They wanted to bring back the Roman Republic, where laws were made by the senate, not by one man. Some believed that the only way to change things was to get rid of Caesar.

THE DAILY ROMAN
16 March 43

CAESAR ASSASSINATED

Last night the whole of Rome was in shock as news spread of the brutal death of our great leader, Gaius Julius Caesar. His bloodstained body was found beneath a statue of his old enemy, Pompey the Great. Perhaps the most shocking news of all is that Senators of Rome, the men whom Caesar had good reason to trust, committed this terrible crime.

It has come to light that the leader of the gang of assassins was none other than Brutus, the man whom Caesar had called a son. It is reported that as Caesar struggled for his life he turned and saw Brutus lift his dagger. At that moment Caesar cried out to Brutus, 'And you too, my child?'. As he did so the life drained from his body and he struggled no more.

There are rumours that Caesar was warned not to attend the meeting that day. A reporter has learned that a soothsayer warned Caesar to 'Beware the **Ides** of March'. A close family member said that Caesar's wife had also warned him not to go because of terrible dreams she had the night before. It is clear now that it was an omen from the gods.

The question on everyone's lips is, 'What now?' Nothing is certain except that today Rome has lost its greatest son.

What do you think?

Do you think the writer of this report was a supporter of Julius Caesar? What makes you think that? Find the evidence in the report.

Fight for power

Julius Caesar was dead, but who would take control of Rome now? There were three men wanted power badly enough to fight for it.

Marcus Brutus

Brutus was one of the leaders of the group who assassinated Caesar.

Mark Antony

Mark Antony served as an officer in Caesar's army. He remained loyal to Caesar.

Octavian

Octavian was a member of Caesar's family. He was named as Caesar's heir.

Emperor Augustus

The armies of all three men fought against each other. By 31 BCE, only one of the three was left alive: Octavian. He later changed his name to Augustus. Julius Caesar, the dictator, was replaced by Augustus, the first Emperor of Rome. The Roman Republic was dead. From now on it would be known as the Roman Empire.

My own research

Emperor Augustus is the only Roman emperor mentioned in the Bible. Read the Gospel of Luke, Chapter 2, verses 1–3 and discover what Emperor Augustus is doing.

Answer on page 32

HOW DO WE KNOW?

The Romans wrote everything down: messages, instructions, ideas, opinions and records of important events. Writing down their many achievements was one way of telling people who came after them just how great the Romans were. For historians this is good news, because the Romans left many different kinds of writing about important people like Julius Caesar. Even Julius Caesar wrote about Julius Caesar!

What people wrote about Julius Caesar

Suetonius was a Roman historian who wrote this about Caesar's appearance.

"Caesar was tall, fair and well-built. His face was broad, his eyes dark and alert. He was very particular about his clothes, careful about shaving and keeping his hair well trimmed. He could not stand his baldness, which his enemies made fun of and so he used to brush his thin hair forward."

Sallust, a Roman historian, who lived at the same time as Caesar, wrote this about him.

"Julius Caesar desired great power, the command of an army and a new war in which his talents might be displayed."

Cicero, a respected senator and the greatest public speaker of his day, wrote these words in a letter to Julius Caesar.

"Your spirit (personality) is much bigger than other people's and it has always burned with a desire to become immortal (remembered for ever)."

A statue of Cicero in Rome.

What was Julius Caesar like?

Consider these facts and what you know about Julius Caesar. Then choose from the adjectives below to best describe what he was like.

1. At his first battle in Gaul, Caesar sent his horse away and stood with his troops ready to fight.

2. Caesar was told to divorce his wife by Sulla, the most powerful man in Rome at the time, because Sulla hated Caesar's father-in-law, Cinna. Julius Caesar refused and escaped from Rome with his wife.

3. When he was 25, Caesar was on his way to Rhodes in Greece when he was captured by sea pirates. After he was freed Caesar hunted down every last pirate and had them all crucified.

brutal   clever   determined   generous   kind   mad   noble   ruthless   selfish   shy   soft   stubborn   trustworthy   weak   wise

FASCINATING FACTS

'I CAME, I SAW, I CONQUERED' IS A VERY FAMOUS QUOTE FROM JULIUS CAESAR. HE WROTE THESE FEW WORDS IN A LETTER TO THE SENATE TO DESCRIBE HIS VERY SWIFT VICTORY OVER AN ENEMY OF ROME.

HISTORY LINKS

NAPOLEON BONAPARTE (1769–1821) WAS ONE OF THE GREATEST GENERALS IN HISTORY. HE BECAME EMPEROR OF FRANCE FROM 1804–15. HIS HERO WAS JULIUS CAESAR. NAPOLEON COPIED CAESAR BY HAVING A BRONZE EAGLE CARRIED HIGH AT THE FRONT OF HIS ARMY. LIKE CAESAR, NAPOLEON WAS A DICTATOR WHO RULED HIS COUNTRY AND MOST OF EUROPE.

CAESAR'S LEGACY

Julius Caesar is the most famous of all Romans but what did he do that has lasted? Here are six ways in which Julius Caesar had an impact on people long after he was dead.

1

By conquering tribes in Gaul, as well as several German tribes, Caesar added lots more territory to lands controlled by Rome. He made the Roman Republic even bigger.

2

Julius Caesar wrote detailed accounts of his many battles, his time in Gaul and his invasion of Britain. They give us a wonderful first-hand account of how events unfolded.

Timothy Dalton playing Julius Caesar in the 1999 series *Cleopatra*.

3

Julius Caesar was a great general. His ideas of how to fight a battle have been used by many different generals throughout history.

4

When Caesar took power away from the senate and became dictator, it changed the way Rome was governed forever. It led to Rome being governed by emperors rather than a council of senators.

This statue of Caesar Augustus is on display in Rome.

5

Caesar gave his name to a new calendar introduced in 46 BCE. It was called the Julian calendar and was very similar to the one we use today, with 365 days in the year, and one extra day every fourth year. The Julian calendar lasted until 1582, when it was replaced by the Gregorian calendar.

An ancient Roman mosaic calendar showing the seasons and months.

6

Julius Caesar was such a great figure in Roman history that all future emperors used his name and called themselves 'Caesar,' starting with Caesar Augustus (above).

Things to do

Rank the six legacies on these pages in order of how long you think they lasted.

Answers on page 32

TIMELINE

100 BCE — JULIUS CAESAR IS BORN

85 BCE — CAESAR BECOMES HEAD OF THE FAMILY WHEN HIS FATHER DIES

80 BCE — CAESAR AWARDED 'CIVIC CROWN' FOR BRAVERY

78 BCE — CAESAR BEGINS SHORT CAREER AS A LAWYER

81-79 BCE — CAESAR SERVES IN ROMAN ARMY IN ASIA MINOR (TURKEY)

76 BCE — ON HIS WAY TO RHODES IN GREECE, CAESAR IS CAPTURED AND RANSOMED BY PIRATES

74 BCE — CAESAR RAISES OWN ARMY TO FIGHT FOR ROME ONCE MORE IN TURKEY

72 BCE — CAESAR SERVES AS A MILITARY TRIBUNE FOR ONE YEAR

67 BCE — CAESAR MARRIES POMPEIA (DIVORCED IN 62 BCE)

69 BCE — CAESAR SERVES AS A QUAESTOR FOR ONE YEAR

65 BCE — CAESAR SERVES AS AN AEDILE FOR ONE YEAR

48 BCE — CAESAR MEETS AND FALLS IN LOVE WITH CLEOPATRA, QUEEN OF EGYPT
•
AT THE BATTLE OF PHARSALUS CAESAR DEFEATS POMPEY'S ARMY AND CLAIMS VICTORY OVER HIS ENEMIES

54 BCE — CAESAR INVADES BRITAIN FOR SECOND TIME BUT RETURNS TO GAUL TO PUT DOWN A REBELLION

55 BCE — CAESAR LEADS FIRST ATTEMPT BY ROME TO INVADE BRITAIN

62 BCE — CAESAR SERVES AS PRAETOR FOR ONE YEAR

59 BCE — CAESAR ELECTED TO SERVE AS A CONSUL OF ROME

58 BCE — CAESAR IS MADE GOVERNOR OF GAUL (FRANCE)

52 BCE — CAESAR FINALLY CONQUERS GAUL BY DEFEATING VERCINGETORIX AT THE BATTLE OF ALESIA

46 BCE — CAESAR INTRODUCES THE 'JULIAN CALENDAR' WHICH IS VERY SIMILAR TO THE ONE WE USE TODAY

49 BCE — CAESAR CROSSES THE RUBICON AND MARCHES ON ROME

44 BCE — CAESAR IS APPOINTED DICTATOR OF ROME FOR LIFE
•
CAESAR IS STABBED TO DEATH BY HIS ENEMIES

27 BCE — OCTAVIAN BECOMES FIRST EVER ROMAN EMPEROR AND CHANGES HIS NAME TO AUGUSTUS.

31 BCE — AT THE BATTLE OF ACTIUM, OCTAVIAN DEFEATS THE FORCES OF MARK ANTONY AND CLEOPATRA

30 BCE — MARK ANTONY AND CLEOPATRA COMMIT SUICIDE

c.4 BCE — BIRTH OF JESUS CHRIST

CE 14 — EMPEROR AUGUSTUS, ADOPTED SON OF JULIUS CAESAR, DIES

GLOSSARY

Assassinate to murder someone for a political reason

Cavalry the part of the army that fought on horses

Civil war a war between groups of people in the same country

Conquer to take over a place by force

Consol elected by the citizens of the Roman Republic; the most powerful people in the senate

Empire a group of countries or states controlled by one ruler

Execute to kill somebody, usually as a legal punishment

Fertile describes rich soil that plants grow well in

General an army leader of very high rank

Governor in the Roman Republic, the person in charge of a city or province

Ides the 15th day of March, May, July and October and the 13th day of other months

Latin the language of ancient Rome and the Roman Empire

Noble somone who was born into a family at the top of society

Philosophy the study of knowledge, truth and human life

Rebellion a violent uprising against a government

Republic a country that is governed by elected politicians and where there is no king or queen.

Senate the most important council in the government

Siege when an army surrounds a place and cuts off its supplies in order to force out its inhabitants

Slaves people who are considered to be owned by others and are forced to work for no pay

Tribe a group of people who live together and share a similar way of life, beliefs and language

Veto the right to stop a law or decision from being made

THE GREAT JULIUS CAESAR QUIZ

1. How old was Julius Caesar when he first invaded Britain?

2. Who did Caesar defeat at the Battle of Alesia?

3. How many soldiers should there have been in a legion?

4. Why was Egypt important to Rome?

5. Where in the world today do senators make laws in a senate?

6. What is a dictator?

7. Where was Julius Caesar born?

8. What was Julius Caesar's main reason for invading Britain?

9. How was Caesar related to Pompey the Great?

WE HAVE REACHED THE EDGE OF THE WORLD.

10. What honour was Julius given when he was 19 years old?

11. What do the letters SPQR mean?

12. Who was the very first Emperor of Rome?

Answers on page 32

INDEX

amphitheatres 10
armour 10, 12
army, Roman 9, 12–15, 25
auxiliaries 12

Battle of Actium 21
Battle of Alesia 15
Battle of Pharsalus 19
Britain, invasion of 5, 7, 16–17, 28

Caesar, Julius
    appearance 6, 9, 26
    captured by pirates 6, 27
    consul 7, 9, 18
    death 4, 5, 12, 24, 25
    dictator 4, 7, 22–25, 29
    early life 4–6
    general 5, 14–19, 28
    governor 7, 14–15, 28
    writings 14–15, 17, 26, 28
calendar, Julian 22, 29
centurions 12
chariot racing 11
Churchill, Winston 14

Cicero 26
Circus Maximus 11
civil war 5, 18–19, 23
Cleopatra 20–21
consuls 7, 8, 9, 18
Crassus 9

Egypt 19, 20–21
Emperor Augustus 21, 25, 29
Emperor Claudius 17
Emperor Napoleon 27
English Civil War 18
entertainment 10–11
equipment, military 13

festivals 8, 10

Gaul 5, 7, 14–15, 16, 18, 27, 28
Germany 14, 28
gladiators 10–11
gods/goddesses 22, 24

King Charles I 18

legionaries 12–13

Marcus Brutus 24, 25
Mark Antony 21, 25

Octavian 21, 25

Pompey 9, 18, 19, 20, 22, 24

Roman Empire 4, 5, 24–25
Roman Republic 4–5, 8, 12, 18, 24–25, 28
Rubicon 18

Sallust 26
senate 4, 5, 7, 8–9, 17, 22, 24, 27, 29
senators 7, 8–9, 17, 19, 22, 23, 24, 26, 29
Seutonius 26
Shakespeare, William 5
soldiers 12–15, 23
SPQR 8
Sulla 27

Vercingetorix 15

weapons 12–15

QUIZ ANSWERS

Things To Do, Page 16: Countries include: Albania, Belgium, Bosnia, Croatia, Cyprus, France, Greece, Italy, Libya, Portugal, Serbia, Spain, Syria, Tunisia, Turkey.

My Own Research, Page 25: Augustus ordered a census of the entire Roman world.

Things to Do, Page 29: 4 (shortest), 1, 6, 5, 2 & 3 (longest)

The Great Julius Caesar Quiz, page 31

1. 45 years old **2.** Vercingetorix, leader of the Gauls **3.** 4,800 men **4.** Egypt provided grain to make bread **5.** The United States of America **6.** Someone with total power **7.** Rome **8.** To get the glory for conquering a new land **9.** Pompey married Caesar's daughter so Caesar was Pompey's father-in-law **10.** Civic Crown **11.** The senate and people of Rome **12.** Augustus, formerly known as Octavian